KILGORE MEMORIAL LIBRARY
6th & Nebraska
York, NE 68467
(402) 363-2620

R.L. 3.8

U.S. Border Patrol

BY KIRSTEN W. LARSON

Amicus High Interest is an imprint of Amicus
P.O. Box 1329, Mankato, MN 56002
www.amicuspublishing.us

Copyright © 2017 Amicus. International copyright reserved in all countries. No part of this book may be reproduced in any form without written permission from the publisher.

Library of Congress Cataloging-in-Publication Data
Names: Larson, Kirsten W., author.
Title: U.S. Border Patrol / by Kirsten W. Larson.
Description: Mankato, MN : Amicus High Interest, an imprint of Amicus, [2017] | Series: Protecting our people | Includes index. | Audience: Grades K-3._
Identifiers: LCCN 2015033741 (print) | LCCN 2015047133 (ebook) | ISBN 9781607539865 (library binding) | ISBN 9781681510262 (ebook) | ISBN 9781681510262 (pdf)
Subjects: LCSH: Border patrols–United States–Juvenile literature. | U.S. Customs and Border Protection–Juvenile literature.
Classification: LCC JV6483 .L38 2017 (print) | LCC JV6483 (ebook) | DDC 363.28/50973-dc23
LC record available at http://lccn.loc.gov/2015033741

Editor: Wendy Dieker
Series Designer: Kathleen Petelinsek
Book Designer: Heather Dreisbach
Photo Researcher: Rebecca Bernin

Photo Credits:Fearnstock/Alamy cover; Bobbie DeHerrera/Stringer/Getty 5; mofles/iStock 6; Associated Press 9, 13, 14, 17, 18-19, 22; Patrick Poendl/iStock 10; Joe Raedle/Staff/Getty 21; Najlah Feanny/CORBIS SABA 24-25; U.S. Immigration and Customs Enforcement/ice.gov 26; David R. Frazier Photolibrary, Inc./Alamy 29

Printed in the United States of America.

10 9 8 7 6 5 4 3 2 1

The author would like to thank the U.S. Border Patrol's Edward Castillo and Ron Vitiello for their technical assistance and expertise.

Table of Contents

A Drug Bust	4
A Day in the Life	8
Learning the Ropes	16
Working with Others	23
Protecting Our People	28
Glossary	30
Read More	31
Websites	31
Index	32

A Drug Bust

In 2015, a big truck crosses into the United States from Mexico. It stops at a **checkpoint**. U.S. Border Patrol agents send the truck through a giant x-ray machine. The scans let the agents see what is inside. The papers say the truck is carrying mattresses. But the x-ray shows something strange. Uh-oh! Agents open up the truck. They get a surprise!

The yellow bar over the truck shows agents what's inside. Are there drugs? Weapons?

U.S. Border Patrol agents stop piles of drugs from coming into the country.

The truck is not filled with mattresses. It is filled with almost 1,300 bags of drugs. Together, the bags of drugs weigh 15 tons (13.6 t). That is the same as three Asian elephants. Yikes! The driver is a **smuggler**! Agents arrest him. They take the drugs away. These brave agents kept illegal drugs out of the United States.

A Day in the Life

All day, people come and go across the U.S. border. Some come to visit for a day or more. Others bring goods to sell. Most people are not doing anything wrong. But sometimes **terrorists** try to sneak in. People try to sneak in guns. Some try to sneak in drugs. To stop these people, agents check everyone at checkpoints.

This agent uses a machine that looks for items hidden in the walls of a truck.

A barbed-wire fence and a wall separate Mexico and the United States in this section of the border.

 Does the Border Patrol watch the entire east and west coasts of the United States?

Border Patrol agents search for signs that people have been in the area.

Q Do people try to cover their tracks when they sneak in?

This drone has cameras and sensors. But no pilot flies it. It is controlled from the ground.

 The U.S. Border Patrol uses Predator Bs. They fly at about 19,000 feet (5,790 m).

To watch very remote places, agents use new technology. Motion sensors lie buried along the border. If someone walks nearby, Border Patrol gets a call.

They also use **drones** to keep watch. These planes do not have pilots, but they do have cameras. The drones alert agents, too.

 What kinds of drones are used?

Some U.S. Border Patrol agents work at remote stations. They do not check cars and trucks. Instead, the station is a base. Agents based there watch the border. There are many stations along the southern border near Mexico. The Canadian border in the north has stations, too. Agents also watch about 2,000 miles (3,220 km) of coastline around Florida and Puerto Rico.

 No. They just watch a small section. Other groups watch the rest of the coasts.

Learning the Ropes

Becoming a U.S. Border Patrol agent is hard. Border Patrol agents must be U.S. citizens. Only people younger than age 37 can apply. They must pass drug tests to prove they have not used illegal drugs. Recruits then take written tests. These tests cover skills needed for the job. One test shows how well they know Spanish. Recruits who pass get an interview.

 Must all agents speak Spanish?

When agents get an alert from a motion sensor or drone, they rush to the scene. They look for the people who set off the sensors. They check for footprints or bent grass. They look for broken branches and cigarette butts. Was someone there? Some agents use dogs to help too. The U.S. Border Patrol has about 800 dogs to sniff out danger.

 Yes. Some walk on upside-down carpet squares. Then they do not leave footprints.

New recruits then go to New Mexico for basic training. It lasts two months. They learn about the law. They work on fitness and shooting guns. They learn off-road driving. They learn how to drive fast too. Zoom!

Recruits who do not speak Spanish learn the language. That training takes 40 more days.

Recruits work hard to get fit during basic training.

Once Border Patrol agents get to their stations, they get on-the-job training. Those working in the north learn how to drive snowmobiles. They learn to track in snow and ice.

Some agents learn to ride horses. Horses can go to places trucks and **ATVs** cannot get to. Horse training takes about four weeks.

 What other vehicles do agents use?

This agent drives a snowmobile in Vermont. It is the best way to get around on snow.

 Some learn how to drive boats. Others fly planes. Some drive ATVs.

In 2011, the Border Patrol captured 1,200 pounds (545 kg) of drugs at the Mexican border in Texas.

Working with Others

The U.S. Border Patrol often works with other U.S. agencies. Together, they keep dangerous people and things out of the United States. The Border Patrol often nabs drugs. They turn them over to the **DEA**. The U.S. Border Patrol also finds weapons. The **ATF** gets those. Still other agencies step in to take the bad guys to jail.

The U.S. Border Patrol also works with local police. If a crook is on the loose, Border Patrol can help. Police describe the person or the car. Agents watch for him. They make sure he does not cross the border. Police also tell the Border Patrol about people who are lost or missing. Agents try to find these people.

Texas police help nab a drug smuggler who wouldn't stop at a checkpoint.

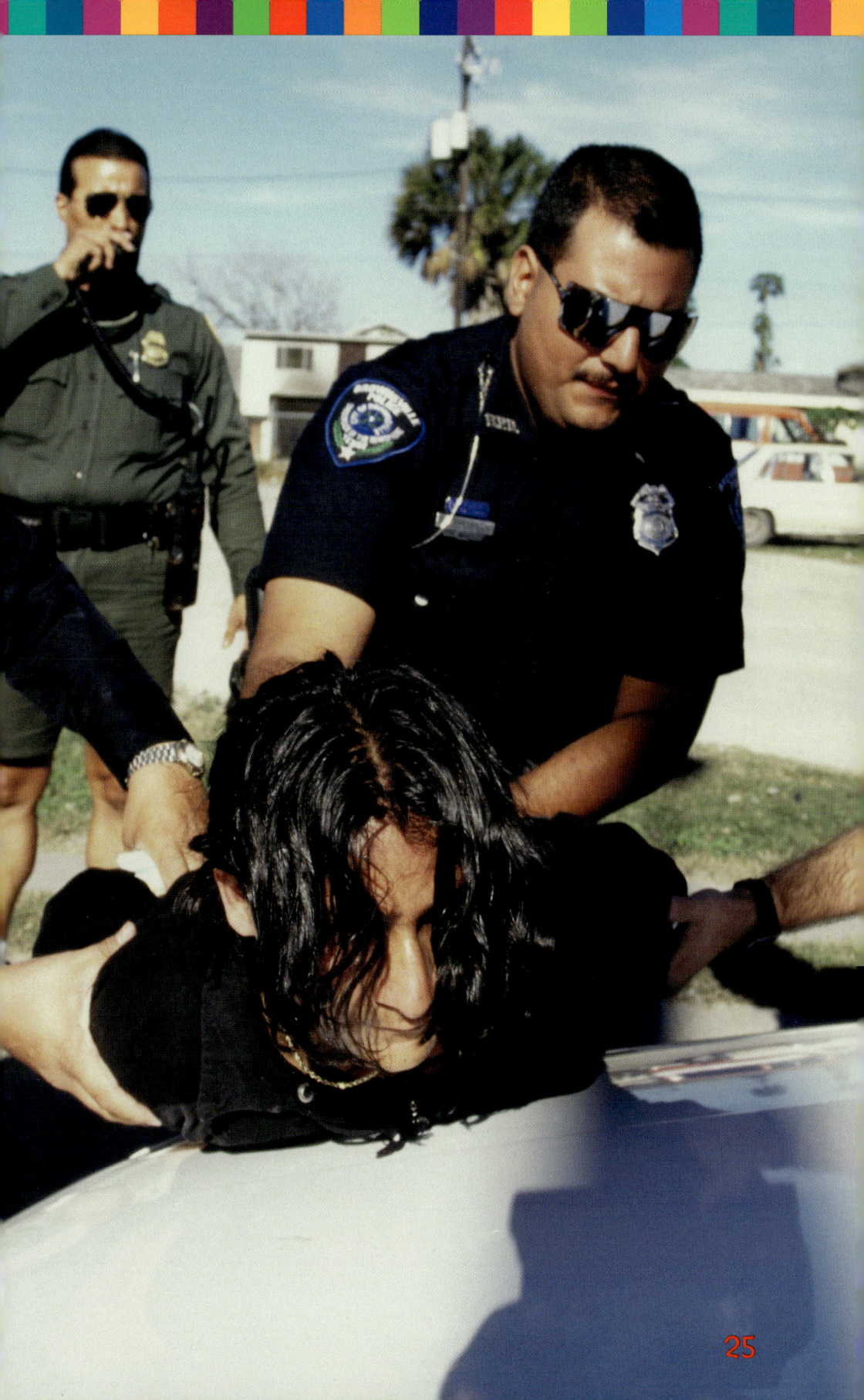

Border Patrol agents have worked with Homeland Security Investigations.

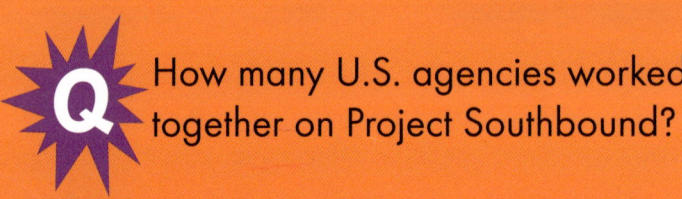

Q How many U.S. agencies worked together on Project Southbound?

26

Border Patrol agents may work on a task force. A task force is a group of people from many agencies. Project Southbound was one task force. The U.S. Border Patrol helped catch more than 600 gang members. They were linked to illegal drugs and other crimes. The task force worked in 179 cities. Some of these cities were along the border.

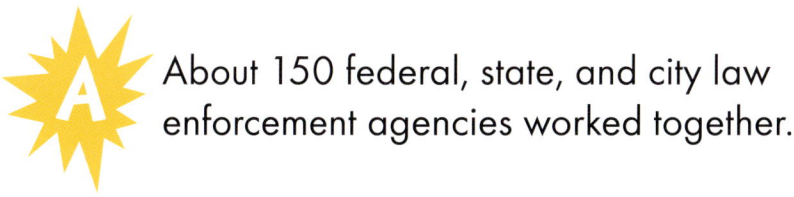
About 150 federal, state, and city law enforcement agencies worked together.

Protecting Our People

Many people want to come to the United States. Some want to work there. Others just want to visit. If people have permission, it is okay.

Yet some criminals try to sneak into the country. They try to bring in dangerous things. When that happens, Border Patrol stops them. Agents keep drugs and weapons away. They keep us safe.

This agent watches the border in California. He works to keep us safe.

Glossary

ATF Short for the Bureau of Alcohol, Tobacco, and Firearms; the government agency that deals with weapons and the illegal trading of alcohol and tobacco.

ATV Short for all-terrain vehicle; a four-wheeler is an ATV.

checkpoint A place where cars and trucks are stopped and checked.

DEA Short for the Drug Enforcement Administration; the government agency that deals with illegal drugs in our country.

drone An aircraft with no pilot on board; drones are often controlled from the ground.

patrol To check an area for safety.

smugglers People who sneak things into or out of a country illegally.

terrorist Someone who uses violence to frighten people.

Read More

Miller, Connie Colwell. *The U.S. Border Patrol: Guarding the Nation.* Mankato, Minn.: Capstone Press, 2008.

Rapine, Dawn. *A Career as a Border Patrol Agent.* New York: PowerKids Press, 2016.

Solway, Andrew. *Graphing Immigration.* Real World Data. Mankato, Minn.: Capstone Press's Heinemann-Raintree, 2010.

Websites

Customs and Border Protection Careers
http://www.cbp.gov/careers

Explore Immigration Data
http://teacher.scholastic.com/activities/immigration/immigration_data/

PBS Kids: Immigration Past and Present
http://pbskids.org/itsmylife/family/immigration/article3.html

Every effort has been made to ensure that these websites are appropriate for children. However, because of the nature of the Internet, it is impossible to guarantee that these sites will remain active indefinitely or that their contents will not be altered.

Index

Bureau of Alcohol Tobacco and Firearms (ATF) 23
Canada 11
checkpoints 4, 8
dogs 15
drones 12, 15
Drug Enforcement Administration (DEA) 23
drugs 7, 8, 16, 23, 27, 28
Florida 11
Mexico 4, 11
motion sensors 12, 15
police 24
Project Southbound 27
Puerto Rico 11
remote stations 11
search mission 15, 20, 24
smugglers 7
Spanish 16, 19
task force 27
terrorists 8
training 16, 19, 20
vehicles 19, 20
weapons 8, 23, 28

About the Author

Kirsten W. Larson has written dozens of books and articles for young people. She lives in Southern California not far from the Mexican border. Visit her website at www.kirsten-w-larson.com.